Are You Coming To My Fiesta?

¿Vas A Venir A Mi Fiesta?

A Bilingual-Spanglish Story

Written by Helina Velazquez-Bailey
Illustrated by Sidney Combs III
Translations by Christopher Nuñez

Copyright @ 2019 HBwritings

All rights reserved.
No part of this book may be reproduced in any manner without written permission of the copyright owner except for the use of quotations in a book review.

First printed edition October 2019.

Written by Helina Velazquez-Bailey
Illustrations by Sidney Combs III
Translation by Christopher Nuñez

ISBN 978-0-9980483-3-8 (Paperback)
ISBN 978-0-9980483-4-5 (Hardcover)

Published by HBwritings
www.Black-Princess.com
Oxnard, Ca. 93030

A big thank you to the Rivera family. I could not have created this book without your love and support. In honor of your rich and beautiful Mexican-American culture, I dedicate this book to all of you.

In memory of my little cousin, Carlos.
Gone but not forgotten.

A special thanks to my primo, Chris, for the tacos. You are an amazing taquero!

Are you coming to my fiesta? Everyone will be there!

Mamá, papá, abuelo, abuela, mis tíos y tías, y mis primos también.

Mom, dad, grandpa, grandma, my uncles, and aunts, and also my cousins.

Vas a venir a mi fiesta? Todos van a estar ahí!

Mamá, papá, mis abuelos, mis tíos y tías, y mis primos también.

I am going to have the best food!

Primo Chris, el taquero, is bringing his taco cart. He will make the sabrosos tacos right in front of you!

Sabroso= delicious   Primo= cousin
El Taquero= taco man

Voy a tener la mejor comida!

Mi primo Chris, el taquero, va a traer su carrito de tacos. Él va a hacer tacos sabrositos justo en frente de ti!

And if you don't want to eat tacos, vamos a bailar.

La musica will be playing in my backyard.

Vamos a bailar= Let's dance

Y si no quieres comer tacos, vamos a bailar.

La música va estar tocando en mi jardín trasero.

I will have the most delicious tres leches cake from the panadería.

**Tres Leches= Three milks
Panaderia= Bakery**

Voy a tener el más delicioso pastel de tres leches de la panadería.

But the best part will be when papá brings out the piñata and hangs it from the tree.

All the kids will line up behind me, because birthday boy always gets to go first!

El mejor parte va a ser al final cuando papá trae la piñata y la cuelga del árbol.

Todos los niños hacen cola atrás de mí porque el cumpleañero siempre va primero!

Mamá will put the blindfold on me and spin me around six times.

One-Two-Three-Four-Five-Six

Mamá me va poner la venda y girarme seis veces.

Uno-Dos-Tres-Cuatro-Cinco-Seis

Everyone will sing and cheer while I try to hit the piñata with my bat.

All the spinning makes me dizzy so I might hit a tío or tía by accident.

Todos van a cantar y torcer mientras yo intento batear la piñata con mi bate de béisbol.

Todas esas vueltas me hacen mareado entonces es posible que bateo un tío o tía por accidente.

There is a loud smack when you hit the piñata with the bat.

Candy and prizes will come rushing out. Everyone will run to collect the candy, scooping it into little bags.

Hay un fuerte ruido cuando pegas la piñata con el bate!

Dulces y premios salen rápidamente. Todos corren para recoger los dulces, poniéndolos en las bolsitas.

But wait, the piñata might not completely break!

Then on to the next one. Another child will spin around and get pushed towards the tree, hoping to smash the piñata into smithereens.

Pero espera, pueda ser que la piñata no quiebre completamente!

Entonces se va al próximo. Otro niño se va a voltear y lo van a empujar hacia el árbol, esperando que quiebre la piñata en pedacitos.

When the piñata is finally broken, the party is over.

Mamá will make me say goodbye to everyone and thank them for the gifts.

Cuando la piñata este finalmente quebrada, la fiesta se termina.

Mamá me manda a despedir todos los convidados y agradecerlos por los regalos.

You don't have to go! You can stay for a little bit longer.

Someone always stays late to help mamá clean.

Tú no tienes que ir! Te puedes quedar por un poco más.

Alguien siempre se queda tarde para ayudar a mi mamá limpiar.

Can you find these items?

- Sombrero
- Maracas
- Taco
- Avocado
- Trumpet
- Present
- Lollipop
- Balloon

Coming Soon!

I Love My Rice

Bilingual Baby

Island Girl

www.ingramcontent.com/pod-product-compliance
Lightning Source LLC
Chambersburg PA
CBHW041442010526
44118CB00003B/151